Tartare à notre façon 21
Tartare poêlé à la plancha 21
Steack à cheval 19
Entrecôte poêlée 300 gr 29
Filet Chateaubriand au poivre
PLATS BASSES CALORIES
Filet de daurade et des haricots verts 22
Tartare de saumon, moutarde à l'estragon 19
Paillard de poulet mariné au citron 22
DESSERTS
le Plateau de pâtisseries 11
Crème brûlée 11 Moelleux au chocolat chaud 11
Fromage blanc au coulis de fruits rouges 11
Salade de fruits frais 11 Café gourmand 11
Sorbets & glaces bio 2 boules 11
Chocolat ou café liégeois 12
Nougat du "Sénéquier" 14

BON APPETIT!

BEST PARISIAN BISTRO RECIPES

FOR FOOD LOVERS

PARIGRAMME

Filet de bar sur peau
Dos de saumon rôti
Tartare de boeuf, frites
Noix de St-Jacques poêlées
Cuisses de grenouilles
Tartiflette de Savoie
Poulet rôti, jus au thym
Cuisse de canard confite
Boeuf bourguignon braisé
Pavé de cœur de rumsteack
Filet de boeuf (250gr.) poêlé
Blanquette de veau
Souris d'agneau braisée
Cheeseburger Maison, frites

Introduction

Those Frogs! Never slow to cut off their kings' heads, to engage in uprisings, or to preach to the whole world on what's right or wrong...

But then again, there's their cuisine. Which is still related to their history when we bear in mind that Parisian restaurants sprouted up in great numbers in the wake of the French Revolution. Indeed, when the domestic staff manning the aristocratic residences that flourished under the pre-revolutionary Ancien Régime suddenly found themselves out of work, they came up with the brilliant idea of setting up their own businesses, offering their talent not just to one master, but to the masses.

Bistros were born later for they only started taking off in Paris after another revolution—the industrial one, this time—in the second half of the 19th century. At this point, impoverished peasants, originally from rural central France, abandoned the countryside that could no longer support them in order to try their luck out in the capital. Here, they opened wood and coal trades, generally attached to wine houses. It wasn't long after that they lengthened their menus to include tasty, hearty and economical dishes. Honest dishes, simpler than the ones served in Paris' restaurants or large cafés. This is how onion soup, eggs en cocotte, stuffed tomatoes, veal blanquette, *steak tartare, crème brûlée* and floating islands gained a following and came to define a "bistro style" destined for wide success. Ever since these humble origins, menus have filled out and opened up to influences from all regions of France, but the bistro style lives on, and all visitors to Paris can still experience it. It is for these visitors—and also others who are yet to stroll along the banks of the Seine—that the following pages gather recipes of the great classics in Parisian bistro cuisine. If it's often said that in France, "everything revolves around the dining table," here is a chance to discover a few reasons why... *Bon appétit!*

There are only
two places in the world
where we can live happy:
in our home
and in Paris.

ERNEST HEMINGWAY

Contents

Starters

Main Dishes

Desserts

STARTERS

Asparagus *with Poached Eggs*

“ ASPERGES AUX ŒUFS POCHÉS ”

SERVE **4**
PREPARATION **10 min**
COOKING **5 min**

4 free-range eggs

1 ¾ lb (800 g) fresh or frozen green asparagus spears

1 tablespoon white vinegar for poaching the eggs

For the vinaigrette:

3 tablespoons olive oil

1 tablespoon balsamic vinegar

Salt and pepper

- Wash the green asparagus, trim off the bottoms of the stems, and remove the small purple “scales.”
- Cook in a frying pan over low heat with a drizzle of olive oil and three tablespoons of water.
- **For the vinaigrette:** mix 3 tablespoons of olive oil, the balsamic vinegar, salt and pepper.

- **For the poached eggs:** Heat water in a saucepan. Add the spoonful of white vinegar, but no salt, to accelerate the coagulation of the egg white.
- Meanwhile, break each egg into a small cup.
- When the water is at boiling point, bring one cup over the water’s surface and flip it over in one fast movement. Repeat with the second cup, at the far side of the saucepan.
- While the eggs cook, draw the egg-white filaments towards the yolk with the help of a skimming ladle, so that they form a cluster.
- After 3 minutes, remove the eggs with the skimming ladle, and place them in a bowl of icy-cold water.
- Cook the two remaining eggs in the same way.
- Arrange the eggs on the asparagus spears and serve with the vinaigrette.

Avocado *with Shrimps*

“ AVOCATS AUX CREVETTES ”

SERVE **4**
PREPARATION **20 min**

4 avocadoes
Juice from ½ lemon
1 shallot
5 oz (150 g) deveined shrimps, cooked and peeled
1 egg yolk
1 ¾ cups (40 cl) oil
2 tablespoons mustard
Parsley and chives
Salt and pepper

- Prepare the mayonnaise: in a bowl, stir together the egg yolk, a large tablespoon of mustard, salt and pepper. Let the mixture rest for about 15 minutes at room temperature. Then, using a mixer set at the lowest speed, add the oil in a slow stream, and blend for about 5 minutes.
- Add the chopped shallot, lemon juice, another spoonful of mustard and the shrimp. Mix gently. Set aside 16 shrimps to decorate the dish.
- To finish, cut the avocadoes in half and remove the pits. Fill each half with mayonnaise and decorate with the remaining shrimps, then the chopped parsley and chives. Keep refrigerated.

Celeriac *Remoulade*

CÉLERI RÉMOULADE

SERVE **4**
PREPARATION **15 min**

1 celeriac
1 egg yolk
1 teaspoon hot mustard
½ pt (¼ l) oil, approx.
2 teaspoons vinegar
Juice from ½ lemon
Salt and pepper

- Peel the celeriac. Grate finely and sprinkle with lemon juice.
- Prepare the remoulade sauce: in a bowl, place the egg yolk, mustard and several drops of vinegar. Make a mayonnaise by pouring the oil in a thin stream while whisking. Thin out the mayonnaise by adding the vinegar, spoonful by spoonful. Season and mix with the grated celeriac. Refrigerate for 2 hours.

Curly Lettuce with Lardons

“ FRISÉE AUX LARDONS ”

SERVE **4**
PREPARATION **5 min**
COOKING **10 min**

1 curly lettuce
7 oz (200 g) smoked lardons or fatty bacon strips
1 bowl walnut kernels
4 very fresh eggs
2 tablespoons vinegar
Salt

For the vinaigrette:
6 tablespoons walnut oil
2 tablespoons walnut or cider vinegar
1 teaspoon mustard
Salt and pepper

- In a saucepan, boil 2 pints (1 liter) of lightly salted water with the vinegar.
- Meanwhile, wash, drain and slice the lettuce.
- **For the vinaigrette:** first mix together the vinegar, mustard, salt and pepper. Add the walnut oil last. Season the lettuce, then distribute it to the individual plates.
- Brown the lardons on a non-stick frying pan without adding any fat, for 2 to 3 minutes.
- To poach the eggs, break them one by one and delicately deposit them into the boiling water. Cook for 3 minutes (4 minutes if you prefer soft-boiled eggs).
- Arrange the eggs on the lettuce, then add the lardons and walnuts. Serve.

Eggs *en Cocotte*

“ ŒUFS COCOTTE ”

SERVE **4**
PREPARATION **5 min**
COOKING **15 min**

4 very fresh eggs
2 tablespoons single cream
Salt and pepper
Chives (optional)

For the bread soldiers:

Butter
4 slices toast

- Generously grease two ramekins. Preheat the oven to 400 °F (200 °C / gas mark 6). Break 2 eggs into each ramekin, taking care not to break the yolks.
- Pour a tablespoon of single cream over each ramekin. Season with salt and pepper.
- Prepare a bain-marie.
- Lower the ramekins into the bain-marie. Place in the oven for about 10 to 15 minutes. Check regularly and remove from the oven when the egg white is just set.
- **For the bread soldiers:** while the eggs cook, prepare the bread soldiers: butter the slices of toast and cut them into sticks.
- Once the eggs are out of the oven, add a pinch of chopped chives if you wish. Serve with the bread soldiers.

Eggs *Mimosa*

“ ŒUFS MIMOSA ”

SERVE **4**
PREPARATION **10 min**

4 eggs
4 teaspoons chopped parsley
1 egg yolk
1 teaspoon mustard
½ cup (12 cl) canola oil
1 green lettuce

- Boil water in a saucepan. Then add the eggs and cook for 10 minutes.
- In the meantime, make a mayonnaise by whisking together an egg yolk with mustard, then slowly adding the oil.
- Remove the shells from the cooked eggs, then slice each in half. Remove the egg yolks and crush them with a fork. Add one half of the crushed egg yolks to the mayonnaise. Fill the egg-white halves with the mayonnaise and scatter with the remaining egg yolks and chopped parsley.
- Serve on a bed of seasoned green lettuce.

Endives *with Roquefort*

“ ENDIVES AU ROQUEFORT ”

SERVE **4**
PREPARATION **15 min**

12 oz (330 g) fromage blanc

3 ½ oz (100 g) Roquefort cheese

Pepper

16 endive leaves

16 walnut kernels (or pine nuts, raisins or hazelnuts)

- Mix the crushed Roquefort with pepper and fromage blanc (dose the fromage blanc according to the desired concentration of Roquefort).
- Bear in mind: if fromage blanc is not available, you can substitute it with Greek yoghurt.
- Place the washed endive leaves on a serving dish, rounded sides downwards.
- Fill the leaves with the Roquefort mixture and sprinkle with walnut kernels.

Lamb's Lettuce *Salad*

“ SALADE DE MÂCHE ”

SERVE **4**
PREPARATION **15 min**

5 oz (150 g) lamb's lettuce
1 ¾ oz (50 g) Roquefort cheese
10 walnut kernels
3 tablespoons walnut oil
1 tablespoon balsamic vinegar
Pepper

- Dice the Roquefort.
- Rinse the lamb's lettuce and drain thoroughly. Put the leaves into a salad bowl. Add the walnut kernels and Roquefort.
- Season with pepper. Add the vinegar and walnut oil just before serving.

Leeks in Vinaigrette

“ POIREAUX VINAIGRETTE ”

SERVE **4**
PREPARATION **5 min**
COOKING **20 min**

4 young leeks

For the vinaigrette:

4 teaspoons peanut oil

2 teaspoons sherry vinegar

1 teaspoon whole-grain mustard

Salt and pepper

- Clean the leeks. Cut off the dark-green ends, then use string to tie the leeks into a small bundle of four.
- Bring to a boil a large pot of salted water.
- Plunge in the bundle of leeks and cook for 20 minutes.
- Drain well and untie the bundle. Place the leeks onto a dish to cool until lukewarm.
- Mix together the sherry vinegar and mustard. Whisk in the oil. Season with salt and pepper.
- Pour the vinaigrette over the leeks and serve lukewarm or cold.

Lentil *Salad*

“ **SALADE DE LENTILLES** ”

SERVE **4**
PREPARATION **10 min**
COOKING **20 min**

9 oz (250 g) green lentils
7 oz (200 g) cherry tomatoes
1 red onion
4 sprigs dill
1 teaspoon mustard
2 teaspoons vinegar
4 teaspoons oil
1 pinch Espelette pepper
Salt and pepper

- Cook the lentils for 20 minutes in salted water. Drain and leave to cool.
- Wash and slice the cherry tomatoes. Slice the onion thinly.
- In a salad bowl, mix the lentils, tomatoes and onion.
- In a separate small bowl, mix the mustard, vinegar and oil with a pinch of salt, pepper and Espelette pepper (season to taste). Add the chopped dill.
- Serve the salad with the vinaigrette.

Marinated Herrings *with Potato Salad*

“ HARENGS MARINÉS POMMES À L’HUILE ”

SERVE **4**
PREPARATION **10 min**

14 oz (400 g) mildly-smoked herring fillets

4 onions

1 large carrot

4 cloves

8 large potatoes

4 sprigs fresh thyme

1 ¾ cups (40 cl) vegetable oil (like sunflower or canola)

Vinegar

- Rinse and drain the herring fillets. Peel the carrot and slice into thin rings. Peel the onions, cut them in half, then slice thinly.
- Cover the bottom of a terrine dish with half the onions and half the carrot. Place on top the herring fillets and cloves. Sprinkle with fresh thyme leaves. Cover with the remaining carrots and onions.
- Add oil until the mixture’s surface is covered. Place a lid on the dish and leave to marinate for 3 to 4 days.
- Accompany with a warm potato salad composed of the potatoes, boiled in water. Season the potatoes with a dribble of vinegar and some of the marinade, including onions and carrots.

Onion Soup

“ SOUPE À L’OIGNON ”

SERVE **4**
PREPARATION **25 min**
COOKING **20 min**

4 onions
1 ¾ oz (50 g) butter
1 tablespoon oil
1 tablespoon flour
1 cup (25 cl) white wine
2 pt (1 l) water
6 slices bread
3 ½ oz (100 g) grated Comté cheese
Salt and pepper

- Peel the onions and chop finely. Cook them in the mixture of butter and oil, until soft and slightly browned.
- Sprinkle the mixture with flour. Add hot water and white wine, then season.
- Cover and simmer gently for 20 minutes.
- Toast the bread. Place one slice each at the bottom of 4 oven-resistant individual bowls.
- Sprinkle with a little grated cheese. Pour the soup over. Sprinkle again with cheese and broil.

Parisian-style Soup

“ POTAGE PARISIEN ”

SERVE **4**
PREPARATION **15 min**
COOKING **20 min**

2 white leek stems
4 large potatoes, e.g. Bintje variety
½ oz (15 g) butter
Crème fraîche
1 sprig parsley
Salt and pepper

- Slice the white leek stems into four lengthwise. Gather together and cut into thin sticks.
- Peel the potatoes. Cut into thick slices roughly 1/5 inch (½ cm) thick, then into sticks, then into cubes.
- Heat the butter in a saucepan over low heat. Brown the leeks over very low heat until they become transparent. Pour in 1 ½ pints (¾ liter) of water.
- Add the potato cubes. Season with salt and pepper. Cook over medium heat for 20 minutes.
- Serve hot with a pot of crème fraîche and decorate with a little parsley.
- Bear in mind: if no crème fraîche is available, you can substitute it with sour cream or else a mixture of buttermilk and cream.

Scallop *Tartare*

“ TARTARE DE SAINT-JACQUES ”

SERVE **4**
PREPARATION **10 min**

12 fresh whole scallops
1 dash olive oil
1 dash balsamic or mango vinegar
Salt and pepper

- Put the scallops in the freezer for 5 to 10 minutes to make them easier to slice.
- Once the 10 minutes are up, remove the scallops from the freezer and slice thinly. Arrange the slices on a plate.
- Add a dash of olive oil, and season to taste with salt and pepper. Finish off with a dash of vinegar.
- For those who appreciate sweet-and-sour associations, scallops go marvelously well with mango.

Tomato *Salad*

“ SALADE DE TOMATES ”

SERVE **4**
PREPARATION **10 min**

8 tomatoes
½ red onion
Several fresh basil leaves
2 tablespoons olive oil
2 dashes cider vinegar
Salt

- Slice the tomatoes into rounds and place into a small salad bowl.
- Add half of the red onion, cut into small pieces. Snip in a few basil leaves.
- Add salt (which will help absorb excess water lost by the tomatoes).
- Stir and refrigerate for about 30 minutes to help the flavors blend together.
- Drizzle over olive oil and cider vinegar, and add a pinch of salt. Serve.

Watercress Soup

“ SOUPE DE CRESSON ”

SERVE **4**
PREPARATION **20 min**
COOKING **40 min**

1 bunch watercress
3 medium-sized potatoes
1 shallot
1 large twig of thyme
1 tablespoon butter
1 stock cube
2 pt (1 l) water (or more depending on the quantity of watercress)
1 twig parsley

- Wash the watercress and remove any stems that are too thick.
- Peel the potatoes and cut into cubes.
- In a large saucepan, heat the butter. When it begins to sizzle (without burning), add the watercress, potatoes, roughly chopped shallot and thyme. Allow the watercress to soften, then add the water and stock cube. The vegetables should be entirely covered by water.
- Turn off the heat when the potatoes are very soft and can be crushed with a wooden spoon.
- When the saucepan's contents have cooled, remove the vegetables and set aside a small quantity of the broth.
- Blend the vegetables with a mixer and add the broth little by little until you obtain the desired consistency. Decorate with a twig of parsley.

MAIN DISHES

Andouillette *with Mustard Sauce*

“ ANDOUILLETTE GRILLÉE SAUCE MOUTARDE ”

SERVE **4**
PREPARATION **15 min**
COOKING **40 min**

4 andouillettes (pork sausage made with tripe)

2 tablespoons whole-grain mustard

1 shallot

3 tablespoons (5 cl) dry white wine

6 tablespoons (10 cl) chicken stock

2/3 cup (15 cl) cream

¾ oz (20 g) butter

Salt and pepper

- Preheat the oven to 410 °F (210 °C / gas mark 7).
- Place the andouillettes on an oven dish and bake for 15 to 20 minutes. Turn over once halfway through the cooking.
- Peel the shallot, then chop finely.
- Heat the butter in a saucepan and sweat the shallot. Add the white wine and leave to reduce completely. Add the chicken stock and cook for 10 minutes.
- Add the mustard and cream and continue cooking for another 5 minutes.
- Plate the andouillettes, cover them with the mustard sauce and serve. Sautéed potatoes and salad make a good accompaniment for the andouillettes.

Beef Bourguignon

SERVE **4**
PREPARATION **1 hour**
COOKING **5 hours**

1 ¼ lb (600 g) stewing beef
4 onions
4 carrots
1 bouquet garni
1 bottle (decent) red wine
3 ½ oz (100 g) butter
Salt and pepper
1 twig parsley

- Cut the beef into 1 inch (3 cm)-long cubes and trim off any large pieces of fat.
- Chop the onions and brown in a frying pan with butter. When transparent, transfer them to a casserole dish, preferably in cast iron.
- Likewise, brown the meat in the frying pan, but in several batches, until all the pieces are cooked. Gradually add to the casserole dish. Don't hesitate to add butter between each batch.
- When all the meat is in the casserole dish, deglaze the frying pan with water or wine. Season the liquid with salt and pepper, and add to the casserole dish.
- Add enough wine to cover the casserole dish's contents and simmer for several hours with the bouquet garni and carrot rounds.
- The next day, simmer the dish for at least 2 hours in several stages, letting it rest between periods of cooking. Add wine or water if necessary. Decorate with a twig of parsley. Serve with fresh pasta.
- The secret is to brown the meat over high heat so that it becomes very dark, almost black. And the more gently the dish simmers, the more sumptuous the results, especially when the cooking is interrupted by rest phases.

Calf's Liver *with Parsley*

“ FOIE DE VEAU PERSILLÉ ”

SERVE **4**
PREPARATION **15 min**
COOKING **5 min**

4 slices calf's liver
1 oz (30 g) flour
2 garlic cloves
½ bunch parsley
7 oz (200 g) tomatoes
¾ oz (20 g) butter
3 tablespoons (5 cl) olive oil
Salt and pepper
Pomegranate seeds

- Peel garlic, then chop with parsley.
- Cut the tomatoes in four and brown in a frying pan with a little olive oil.
- Flour the slices of calf's liver and season with salt and pepper.
- In a frying pan with a dash of olive oil, brown the veal liver slices on both sides. Lower the heat and add the butter, chopped garlic and parsley. Spoon the parsley butter over the slices of liver.
- Serve with steamed potatoes. And decorate with a handful of pomegranate seeds.

Choucroute

SERVE **4**
PREPARATION **35 min**
COOKING **2 ½ hours**

2 lb (1 kg) raw sauerkraut
2 onions
1 ¾ oz (50 g) lard, goose fat or butter
1 bay leaf
4 cloves
10 juniper berries
3 garlic cloves
1 lb (500 g) pork ribs
10 ½ oz (300 g) pork belly
5 oz (150 g) smoked bacon
6 Montbéliard (thick smoked) sausages
6 Strasbourg (thinner smoked) sausages
1 ½ pt (75 cl) Sylvaner (Alsatian white wine)
2 lb (1 kg) potatoes
Salt and pepper

- Rinse the sauerkraut thoroughly in cold water and drain.
- Peel and chop the onions. Peel the garlic cloves.
- Cut into slices the pork ribs, pork belly and smoked bacon.
- In a casserole dish or cooking pot, melt the lard, goose fat or butter, and brown the onions.
- Add a quarter of the sauerkraut and season with the garlic cloves, bay leaf, cloves and juniper berries. Place on top the pork ribs, pork belly and smoked bacon. Add the rest of the sauerkraut and sprinkle over the Sylvaner. Season with salt and pepper.
- Cover and stew over low heat for at least 2 hours.
- Towards the end of the cooking time, simmer water in a large saucepan, without letting it boil.
- Prick holes in the Strasbourg and Montbéliard sausages, and cook them in the simmering water: 30 minutes for the Montbéliards, and 15 minutes for the Strasbourgs.
- Boil or steam potatoes in another saucepan.
- Serve the choucroute in a large serving dish, arranging the meats and potatoes on top of the sauerkraut.

Coq au Vin

SERVE **4**
PREPARATION **30 min**
COOKING **2 ¾ hours**

1 cock (or chicken) weighing roughly 6 lb (3 kg), cut into pieces
½ bottle full-bodied red wine
4 ½ oz (130 g) bacon strips
4 ½ oz (130 g) button mushrooms
½ chopped onion
1 carrot sliced into rounds
1 garlic clove
½ bouquet garni
½ tablespoon peppercorns
1 cup (25 cl) veal stock
1 ½ tablespoons (2 ½ cl) cognac
1 ½ tablespoons oil
½ tablespoon flour
Salt and pepper

- The day before: marinate the poultry by placing it in a large bowl with the onion and carrot. Pour in the wine, add the bouquet garni and peppercorns. Cover and leave overnight in the refrigerator (or all day if you wish to prepare it for the evening meal).
- On the day: drain the poultry and vegetables, and sponge dry with kitchen paper.
- Filter the marinade and set it aside.
- Heat the oil in a cooking pot. Add the pieces of poultry and brown them on every side.
- Remove the browned meat from the cooking pot, and replace it with the vegetables. Brown the vegetables over low heat for 5 minutes. Sprinkle over the flour, and mix well to cover the vegetables thoroughly.
- Put the poultry pieces back in the cooking pot, add the crushed garlic clove. Heat the cognac, pour it in and flambé.
- Wet the mixture with the wine from the marinade, and add the veal stock. Season with salt and pepper. Bring to a boil, then cover and lower the heat. Leave to simmer over low heat for two and a half hours.
- Chop the mushrooms finely. Brown them in a frying pan with the bacon strips for 5 to 10 minutes. Add them to the cooking pot 15 minutes before serving. Taste and season again if necessary.
- Serve with fresh pasta.

Croque-Monsieur

SERVE **4**
PREPARATION **10 min**
COOKING **10 min**

8 slices white bread
3 ½ oz (100 g) grated cheese (e.g. gruyere)
1 ¾ cups (40 cl) thick crème fraîche (preferably fat-reduced)
4 slices cooked ham
A little grated nutmeg

- Preheat the broiler, or else the oven at maximum temperature if you have no broiler.
- Stack the slices of ham in a pile. Place on top a slice of bread and trim the ham around the bread's outline. Not only will this improve the sandwiches' presentation, but it will also help them to stay together.
- Lay out the slices of bread on your worktop. Spread with crème fraîche—more or less to suit your taste. Sprinkle over with grated nutmeg, then add the grated cheese.
- On half of the bread slices, place a slice (or two) of ham. Add a little crème fraîche and grated cheese.
- Place one ham-less slice of bread on top of a slice with ham. Press down lightly to seal them together and prevent slippage during the cooking. Repeat with the remaining slices.
- Place under the broiler (at the maximum temperature) for 5 minutes, or about 10 minutes if using the oven.

Endives *with Ham*

“ ENDIVES AU JAMBON ”

SERVE **4**
PREPARATION **20 min**
COOKING **45 min**

8 endives
8 slices ham
Grated cheese

For the béchamel:
1 pt (½ l) milk
1 oz (30 g) flour
1 oz (30 g) butter
1 teaspoon nutmeg
Salt and pepper

- **For the béchamel:** melt the butter in a saucepan over low heat, then add the flour. Stir while cooking. Add the milk little by little and continue mixing to obtain a smooth and uniform consistency. Add salt, pepper and nutmeg.
- Cook the endives in boiling water for 10 minutes.
- Roll each endive in a slice of ham and place in a greased oven dish.
- Fill the dish with the béchamel sauce. Sprinkle with grated cheese. Bake in the oven at 350 °F (180 °C / gas mark 6) for 20 minutes.

French Fries or Pont Neuf Potatoes

“ FRITES OU POMMES PONT-NEUF ”

SERVE **4**
PREPARATION **15 min**
COOKING **15 min**

1 ¾ lb (800 g) firm-fleshed potatoes
4 pt (2 l) peanut oil
Salt

- Pour the oil into a deep fryer over medium heat. The oil's temperature should reach approximately 320 °F (160 °C / gas mark 5).
- Carefully peel the potatoes. Cut into square-based sticks, roughly 2 ¾ inches (7 cm) long and 1/3 inch (1 cm) thick.
- Little by little, add the potatoes to a bowl of very cold water, then dry on a dish towel. Then plunge the potatoes into the deep fryer and leave to cook for 7 minutes. Remove and drain.
- Just before serving, increase the oil's temperature to 350 °F (180 °C / gas mark 6) and plunge the potatoes back in for 2 to 3 minutes until golden in color.
- Place the potatoes on a warmed dish and season with salt. Serve hot.

French Shepherd's Pie

“ HACHIS PARMENTIER ”

SERVE **4**
PREPARATION **10 min**
COOKING **1 hour**

1 ¾ lb (800 g) potatoes
2/3 cup (15 cl) milk
1 tablespoon cream
1 ½ oz (40 g) butter
3 oz (80 g) grated cheese (e.g. gruyere)
Salt and pepper
Nutmeg (optional)
14 oz (400 g) minced beef
1 onion
1 garlic clove
1 carrot
¾ oz (25 g) butter
Salt and pepper

- Chop the onion and garlic. Peel the carrot and dice finely. Peel the potatoes and cut into small pieces.
- Cook the potatoes in salted water or milk (watch that the milk doesn't boil over) for around 30 minutes.
- Cook the carrots in the butter for 1 minute, then add the onion and garlic. Leave to cook for another 1 minute.
- Add the meat. Season with salt and pepper, and cook while stirring for 10 minutes.
- Mash the potatoes (with a potato masher or food mill) and add the butter, milk, cream and plenty of salt. Mix quickly.
- Place the meat in a gratin dish and cover with the mashed potato. Top with the grated cheese.
- Bake in oven at 400 °F (200 °C / gas mark 7) for 10 minutes, then broil for 2 minutes before serving.

Gratin *Dauphinois*

SERVE **4**
PREPARATION **25 min**
COOKING **1 hour**

2 lb (1 kg) potatoes
1 ½ garlic clove
¾ cup (20 cl) cream
2 ¼ oz (65 g) butter
2 pt (1 l) milk
1 pinch nutmeg
Salt and pepper

- Peel and wash the potatoes, then cut into thin rounds. Careful not to wash them AFTER cutting because the potato starch is needed to obtain the right consistency.
- Chop the garlic very finely.
- In a saucepan, bring to a boil the milk, garlic, salt, pepper and nutmeg, then add the potatoes and leave to cook for 10 to 15 minutes (depending on how firm they are).
- Preheat the oven to 350 °F (180 °C / gas mark 6) and grease a gratin dish.
- Put the drained potatoes in the gratin dish. Cover with cream, then place small nobs of butter on top.
- Bake in the oven for 1 hour, then serve with a green salad.

Hanger Steak *with Shallots*

“ ONGLET POÊLÉ À L’ÉCHALOTE ”

SERVE **4**
PREPARATION **5 min**
COOKING **5 min**

4 hanger steaks

8 shallots

5 tablespoons (80 ml) dry white wine

4 tablespoons (60 ml) veal stock

3 ½ oz (100 g) + 2 tablespoons butter

Salt and pepper

- Finely chop the shallots.
- Season the hanger steaks with salt and pepper. Sear both sides of each steak over high heat in a frying pan with the 2 tablespoons of butter. The meat should be removed from the pan quickly and kept warm.
- In the same frying pan, cook the shallots over low heat. When they have caramelized, add the wine and bring to a boil until the cooking juices have completely evaporated. Add the veal stock and bring to a boil. Thicken the sauce by whisking in the rest of the cold butter.
- Serve the meat immediately, accompanied by the sauce, French fries and salad.

Lamb Navarin with Vegetables

“ NAVARIN D'AGNEAU AUX LÉGUMES ”

SERVE **4**
PREPARATION **30 min**
COOKING **1 ½ hour**

2 lb (1 kg) neck of lamb and lamb shoulder
7 oz (200 g) carrots
7 oz (200 g) green beans
7 oz (200 g) peas
7 oz (200 g) new potatoes
2 garlic cloves
1 lb (500 g) tomatoes
1 bouquet garni
1 tablespoon oil
1 chicken stock cube
Salt and pepper

- Cut the meat into pieces. Heat a little oil in a frying pan over medium heat and add the meat. Brown every surface.
- When browned, place the meat in a casserole dish and add water to cover the meat. Add the bouquet garni, the tomatoes cut into pieces and the peeled garlic.
- Dilute the stock cube in a little water and pour into the casserole dish. Season with salt and pepper. Cook over low heat for 1 hour.
- Peel the carrots and potatoes, and cut into pieces. Add them to the meat after 1 hour of cooking.
- Shell the peas and cook them with the green beans in salted water for 10 minutes.
- Check the lamb—the meat should be tender. Remove the pieces of lamb from the casserole dish and place into a serving dish. Arrange the vegetables around the meat.
- To finish, spoon the sauce over the navarin.

Mussels *in White Wine*

“ MOULES MARINIÈRE ”

SERVE **4**
PREPARATION **10 min**
COOKING **15 min**

Roughly 8 lb (4 kg) mussels (2 lb / 1 kg per person)

3 onions

¾ cup (20 cl) white wine

1 bouquet garni

2 garlic cloves

Chopped parsley

1 ¾ oz (50 g) butter

Pepper

- In a cooking pot, melt the butter and add the chopped onions, crushed garlic cloves and bouquet garni. Sweat for 5 minutes. Add the mussels, washed beforehand. Pour in the white wine and add pepper.
- Cook covered for 8 to 10 minutes, stirring from time to time, until the mussel shells have opened. Sprinkle with chopped parsley before serving.

Pot-au-Feu

SERVE **4**
PREPARATION **30 min**
COOKING **4 hours**

3 lb (1 ½ kg) beef: chuck steak, topside, rump steak and oxtail in equal quantities
1 marrowbone
4 leeks
4 carrots
4 potatoes
1 celery stalk
2 onions
1 garlic clove
1 bouquet garni (parsley, thyme, bay leaf)
2 cloves
Sea salt
6 black peppercorns

- Bind the pieces of meat with string so that they keep their shape while cooking. If using oxtail, cut into segments.
- Peel and wash the carrots, leeks, potatoes and celery stalk.
- Prick one onion with the cloves. Brown the second onion dry in the oven: it will bring color to the broth.
- Place into a cooking pot all the pieces of meat along with the marrowbone, wrapped in cheesecloth beforehand to prevent the marrow from dispersing. Add 10 pints (5 liters) of cold water.
- Season with sea salt. Bring to a boil and leave to boil, taking care to skim the top until no more foam forms.
- Add the onions, carrots, potatoes, leeks (tied into a bundle), celery stalk, garlic and bouquet garni (tied together with string beforehand). Add 6 peppercorns.
- Bring to a boil again, then leave to cook over very low heat, covered (while leaving a small vent to allow steam to escape), for at least 4 hours.
- While cooking, use a ladle to remove any grease that collects on the surface.
- The pot-au-feu broth can be eaten hot or lukewarm. It can also be used as the base of various soups.
- Remove the meat and vegetables from the broth and arrange them on a warmed serving dish.
- Serve immediately, with gherkins, sea salt and hot mustard.

Quenelles *with Nantua Sauce*

“ QUENELLES SAUCE NANTUA ”

SERVE **4**
PREPARATION **10 min**
COOKING **45 min**

8 pike quenelles
1 pt (50 cl) milk
¾ cup (20 cl) thick crème fraîche
1 small pot seafood butter
1 ½ oz (40 g) butter
1 tablespoon flour
1 pinch nutmeg
Salt and pepper

- Preheat the oven to 350 °F (180 °C / gas mark 6).
- Melt the butter in a saucepan over low heat. Add the flour, stir and cook for a few minutes.
- Pour in the cold milk gradually while whisking to prevent lumps from forming. Cook for 10 minutes over low heat while stirring, to thicken the béchamel. Then mix in the crème fraîche, seafood butter, salt, pepper and nutmeg.
- Grease an ovenproof dish. Put in the quenelles and pour the sauce over them.
- Bake for about 20 minutes. The quenelles are ready when they are puffed up and golden. Serve with rice.

Rabbit *with Mustard*

“ LAPIN À LA MOUTARDE ”

SERVE **4**
PREPARATION **15 min**
COOKING **1 hour**

1 rabbit, cut into pieces
1 onion
8 tablespoons mustard
1 shallot
1 pt (50 cl) dry white wine
10 ½ oz (300 g) button mushrooms
1 ¾ oz (50 g) cornstarch
Salt and pepper
Parsley

- Sprinkle the rabbit pieces with salt and pepper and cover them with hot mustard (add the mustard liberally as it loses its heat when it cooks). Then flour the pieces.
- Brown the rabbit with a little oil in a stew pot over medium heat, then remove the meat and set aside.
- Sweat the aromatics (shallots, onion and parsley) in the stew pot over low heat. Stir in any rabbit cooking juices at the bottom of the pot.
- Put the rabbit pieces (except the liver) back into the stew pot, and add the white wine. Season with salt and pepper. Cook for roughly one hour over low heat.
- A quarter of an hour before the end of the cooking, add the quartered mushrooms and the rabbit's liver.
- Before plating the rabbit, check the seasoning and thicken the sauce with cornstarch. Serve with fresh pasta.

Rib Steak *with Béarnaise Sauce*

“ ENTRECÔTE BÉARNAISE ”

SERVE **4**
PREPARATION **20 min**
COOKING **10 min**

4 rib steaks

For the béarnaise sauce:

2 egg yolks
3 ½ tablespoons white wine
2 tablespoons wine vinegar
2 tablespoons fresh tarragon
1 shallot, very finely chopped
3 ½ oz (100 g) butter
Salt and pepper

- Lightly oil the steaks. Place on a hot grill to obtain crisscross sear marks on both sides, then season. Cook 5 to 10 minutes, depending on how well done you want the meat.
- **For the béarnaise sauce:** pour the white wine and vinegar into a saucepan, and add the tarragon, salt, pepper and chopped shallots.
- Cook for about 10 minutes to reduce a little.
- Remove from the heat and wait a few minutes. Add the egg yolks and beat.
- Place the saucepan back over low heat and mix continuously to thicken the béarnaise. Bear in mind: egg yolks cook at 158 °F (70 °C / gas mark 2), so mix thoroughly and watch the heat.
- When a thick sauce has formed, remove from the heat and add the cold butter cut into small pieces, piece by piece.
- Place each steak on a plate and serve the sauce separately in a sauce boat.

Roast Chicken *with French Fries*

“ POULET FRITES ”

SERVE **4**
PREPARATION **30 min**
COOKING **1 ½ hour**

- 1 chicken weighing 3 lb (1 ½ kg)
- 2 lb (1 kg) potatoes (preferably Bintje variety)
- 1 bunch fresh thyme
- 2 tablespoons mustard
- 4 tablespoons sunflower oil
- Salt and pepper

- Preheat the oven to 320 °F (160 °C / gas mark 5) using the convection setting. Season the chicken (inside and outside) with salt and pepper. Combine the mustard with 2 tablespoons of sunflower oil. Use a brush to cover the chicken with the mustard mixture, then scatter with thyme. Place the chicken belly-side down into an oven dish. Drizzle over 2 tablespoons of sunflower oil. Bake for 1 ½ hour. Every 20 minutes, turn the chicken 90° on its side and cover with more mustard and thyme.
- Heat oil in the deep fryer to 320 °F (160 °C). Peel the potatoes and cut into 1/6 inch (4 mm)-side sticks. Set aside -in cold water to prevent them from darkening in color. Drain, rinse and sponge the potato sticks dry with a clean dishcloth. Plunge the fries into the oil in small batches for 4 minutes. Drain and set aside the fries without packing them down.
- Several minutes before serving, raise the oil's temperature to 350 °F (180 °C / gas mark 6) and finish off the fries by cooking them in the oil for about 5 minutes. Drain them on kitchen paper, then transfer to a large bowl containing salt, tossing to cover the potatoes evenly. The two-step frying process produces fries that are golden and crispy on the outside, soft on the inside.

Roast Lamb *with Garlic*

“ GIGOT À L’AIL ”

SERVE **4**
PREPARATION **10 min**
COOKING **45 min**

1 leg of lamb
1 ½ twigs fresh rosemary
1 ½ garlic cloves (vary to suit taste)
1 tablespoon sea salt
Goose or duck fat

- Preheat the oven to 410 °F (210 °C / gas mark 7).
- Prepare the lamb by using a knife to trim off fat on the leg’s surface to reveal the red flesh.
- Make a paste with the goose or duck fat, crushed garlic and sea salt. Rub the paste into the lamb flesh, massaging it in.
- Put in the oven with the rosemary and moisten every half hour with a mixture of hot water and goose or duck fat.
- Garlic fans may like to place a few unpeeled garlic cloves on the bottom of the oven dish.
- Serve with fresh green beans tossed with garlic and parsley, or sautéed potatoes with parsley.

Salted Pork with Lentils

“ PETIT SALÉ AUX LENTILLES ”

SERVE **4**
PREPARATION **10 min**
COOKING **2 hours**

1 ¾ lb (800 g) petit salé (various cuts of salted pork, preserved in brine, including pork shoulder, loin, spare ribs)

10 ½ oz (300 g) green lentils

5 carrots

1 big onion

1 bouquet garni (thyme, bay leaf, rosemary)

3 cloves

Salt and pepper

- The night before: soak the lentils, and desalt the meat in a large bowl of water.
- In a large casserole dish, place the onion, peeled and pricked with the cloves, along with the bouquet garni and the meat. Add enough water to cover the contents and cook over low heat for 2 hours.
- 30 minutes before the end of the cooking time, add the lentils and the carrots cut into pieces.
- When cooked, drain the lentils. Remove the bouquet garni and the clove-pricked onion.
- Transfer the lentils and carrots to a deep serving dish. Arrange the pieces of meat on top and add a few spoonfuls of the cooking juices. Season with salt and pepper at the last moment.

Skate *with Capers*

“ RAIE AUX CÂPRES ”

SERVE **4**
PREPARATION **5 min**
COOKING **15 min**

4 skinned skate wings

6 tablespoons (10 cl) white vinegar

1 bay leaf

1 sprig thyme

Peppercorns

1 teaspoon sea salt

Several juniper berries

For the sauce:

2 oz (60 g) unsalted butter

1 ½ oz (40 g) lightly salted butter

1 teaspoon lemon juice

2 tablespoons drained capers

2 twigs flat-leaf parsley

- Place, in a large saucepan of cold water, the skate wings, vinegar, bay leaf, thyme, peppercorns and sea salt.
- Heat gently to simmering point and cook for 15 minutes without boiling.

For the sauce:

- Chop the parsley.
- Melt the unsalted butter in a saucepan for 1 to 2 minutes, then add the lightly salted butter.
- Once the butter has melted, add the lemon juice, capers and chopped parsley, then remove from heat.
- Drain the skate wings. Serve with the sauce.

Sole *Meunière*

SERVE **4**
PREPARATION **10 min**
COOKING **10 min**

4 soles
1 lemon
1 ¾ oz (50 g) flour
1 ¾ oz (50 g) butter
2 tablespoons oil
Salt and pepper

- Remove the soles' brown skin.
- In a dish, flour both sides of the soles, seasoned with salt and pepper.
- In a frying pan, heat the oil. When it is hot, start cooking the fish. When the first side of the fish is golden, turn it over.
- Set aside the cooked fish and remove the oil from the pan.
- Place the pan back on the heat and add the butter. Place the soles back in the pan and leave them to keep cooking. When the butter is a hazelnut color, take the pan off the heat immediately so that the sauce doesn't turn brown.
- Deglaze with lemon juice—the butter will form large bubbles. Plate immediately and serve, accompanied with steamed potatoes.

Steak *Tartare*

SERVE **4**
PREPARATION **20 min**

1 lb (500 g) fresh beef fillet
1 egg yolk (+ 4 for the garnish)
2 teaspoons Dijon mustard
2 tablespoons chopped onions
2 tablespoons chopped capers
2 teaspoons Worcestershire sauce
2 tablespoons tomato ketchup
1 drop Tabasco
Salt and pepper
4 tablespoons olive oil
2 teaspoons chopped flat-leaf parsley

- With a knife, dice the meat extremely finely into a brunoise.
- In a bowl, mix the egg yolk, Dijon mustard, onion, capers, Worcestershire sauce, tomato ketchup, Tabasco, salt and pepper. Add the olive oil while stirring with a whisk.
- Combine the meat to the sauce, then mix in the parsley. Check the seasoning.
- Refrigerate or serve immediately.
- Bear in mind: this dish cannot be prepared more than 2 hours ahead and should always be stored refrigerated. It is traditionally garnished with a raw egg yolk and served with fries as a main dish. Sirloin or flank steak can be used—in any case the meat should be lean.

Stuffed Cabbage

“CHOU FARCI”

SERVE **4**
PREPARATION **25 min**
COOKING **1 ½ hour**

1 green cabbage
14 oz (400 g) sausage mince
2 eggs
2 carrots
7 oz (200 g) button mushrooms
5 tablespoons (7 cl) stock
4 tomatoes
3 slices white bread
½ glass milk
2 cloves garlic
1 large onion
3 tablespoons butter
Salt and pepper

- Prepare the stuffing: combine the sausage mince, eggs and white bread (soaked in milk beforehand), chopped garlic, salt and pepper. Combine until the mixture is homogenous.
- Boil water in a large pot. Wash the cabbage. When the water is at boiling point, dip the cabbage head down into the bubbling water, for 2 to 3 minutes.
- Then cut out the cabbage heart (save it for a soup). Insert stuffing between the cabbage leaves. Fold the leaves down, one by one, tightly around the stuffing. Bind the cabbage with string.
- Place the butter into a cast-iron casserole dish. Brown the cabbage all over its surface. Add the chopped onion, carrots sliced into rounds and tomatoes, peeled and sliced into four. Pour over the stock. Season with salt and pepper. Cover and leave to cook for 90 minutes, turning over the cabbage from time to time.
- Clean the mushrooms and cut them into four, then brown in oil. Add at the end to make the dish even more appealing.

Stuffed Tomatoes

“ TOMATES FARCIES ”

SERVE **4**
PREPARATION **20 min**
COOKING **1 hour**

- 4 large tomatoes suitable for stuffing
- 1 lb (500 g) sausage mince
- 3 onions
- 2 garlic cloves
- 1 twig thyme
- 6 twigs parsley
- ¾ oz (20 g) butter
- Salt and pepper

- Peel and chop the onions and garlic cloves.
- Combine half of the onions with the sausage mince. Add garlic, salt, pepper and a little parsley.
- Slice off the tops of the tomatoes and empty out their flesh. Season their insides with salt and pepper. Fill them with the stuffing and replace the tops of the tomatoes.
- Add the rest of the onions to the tomato flesh in an oven dish.
- Place the stuffed tomatoes into the dish. Sprinkle with a little thyme and top each tomato with a nob of butter.
- Bake in the oven heated to 350 °F (180 °C / gas mark 6) for around 1 hour.
- Serve with rice.

Tournedos *Rossini*

SERVE **4**
PREPARATION **20 min**
COOKING **5 min**

4 beef tournedos (round tenderloin steaks)
4 slices stale bread
3 ½ oz (100 g) butter
4 tablespoons (6 cl) cognac
4 tablespoons (6 cl) Madeira wine
¾ cup (20 cl) thick crème fraîche
4 generous slices foie gras
Salt and pepper

- Cut the bread into rounds the same size as the tournedos. Sear the pieces of meat on both sides in 1 ¾ oz (50 g) butter in a frying pan. Set aside.
- Heat the cognac in a small saucepan.
- Melt the rest of the butter in the frying pan until it takes on a hazelnut color. Add the tournedos and brown over high heat for 3 to 5 minutes depending on the desired cooking, turning them over in the middle of the cooking. Season with salt and pepper, and flambé with the cognac.
- Put the rounds of bread on the warmed serving plates, then place a tournedos on each and keep warm in the oven at 210 °F (100 °C / gas mark 3) for example.
- Pour the Madeira wine into the frying pan to deglaze and add the crème fraîche. Season with salt and pepper.
- Thicken the sauce over low heat by stirring well.
- Place a slice of foie gras on each tournedos and cover with sauce.
- Serve immediately, for example with fried mushrooms and a potato and celeriac mash.

Veal *Blanquette*

“ BLANQUETTE DE VEAU ”

SERVE **4**
PREPARATION **30 min**
COOKING **2 hours**

2 lb (1 kg) boneless veal, cut into chunks
2 carrots
1 yellow onion
1 small box of mushrooms (sliced)
1 small pot of crème fraîche
Lemon
1 egg yolk
1 cup (25 cl) white wine
1 vegetable stock cube
1 chicken stock cube
2 tablespoons flour
Salt and pepper
1 twig parsley

- Cook the veal pieces with a little unsalted butter until they brown slightly.
- Sprinkle with the flour. Mix well.
- Add 2 to 3 glasses of water, the stock cubes, the wine, and stir. Add water to cover if necessary.
- Slice the carrots into rounds and chop the onion, then add to the meat, along with the mushrooms.
- Leave to simmer over very low heat for around 1 ½ to 2 hours, stirring occasionally.
- If necessary, add water from time to time.
- In a bowl, mix together well the crème fraîche, egg yolk and lemon juice. Add this mixture to the meat at the last moment and stir thoroughly. Decorate with a sprig of parsley and serve immediately with rice.

Veal *Paupiettes*

"PAUPIETTES DE VEAU"

SERVE **4**
PREPARATION **15 min**
COOKING **30 min**

4 veal paupiettes (thin slice of pounded veal wrapped around a forcemeat stuffing)
2 garlic cloves
2 tablespoons olive oil
4 tablespoons veal stock
1 cup (25 cl) white wine
1 cup (25 cl) water
2 tablespoons hot mustard
2 tablespoons balsamic vinegar

- In a frying pan over medium heat, heat the olive oil and add the finely chopped garlic cloves.
- When the pan is well heated, put in the paupiettes and brown for several minutes on every side.
- When all the surfaces are slightly browned, add the veal stock, then the white wine and water.
- Next add the mustard and balsamic vinegar, and mix well, turning over the paupiettes so that they soak up the sauce.
- Cook for 5 minutes over medium heat so that the alcohol in the white wine evaporates, then adjust to low heat and cover.
- Simmer for about 20 minutes, turning over the paupiettes from time to time. Serve with green beans or steamed potatoes.

Chocolat
à l'ancienne
Thés
Mariage Frères
Cappuccino

DESSERTS

Bourdaloue Tart

“ TARTE BOURDALOUE ”

SERVE **4**
PREPARATION **30 min**
COOKING **40 min**

4 pear halves in syrup
Toasted almond flakes

For the shortcrust pastry:

3 ½ oz (100 g) softened butter
5 oz (150 g) flour
1 pinch salt
2 tablespoons sugar
5 tablespoons cold water

For the almond cream:

2 oz (60 g) butter
1 egg
2 oz (60 g) sugar
2 ¾ oz (80 g) almond meal

- **For the shortcrust pastry:** place the flour into a large bowl, then add the salt, sugar and butter, cut into pieces. Quickly blend together. Add the cold water and combine. Knead the dough until it becomes supple. Form a ball, then cover with plastic wrap and leave to rest for at least 30 minutes.
- **For the almond cream:** beat the egg, butter and sugar until you obtain a smooth cream. Add the almond meal and mix well.
- Preheat the oven to 350 °F (180 °C / gas mark 6). Place the dough, rolled out on a piece of greaseproof paper and pricked with a fork, into a pie dish. Pour the almond cream on top and spread evenly. Arrange the pear halves on top. Each pear half should be sliced beforehand into three without severing the segments, so that the piece can be fanned out.
- Bake for at least 30 minutes.
- After taking the pie out of the oven, scatter with flaked almonds. Serve the pie when it has cooled completely.

Café *Liégeois*

SERVE **4**
PREPARATION **10 min**

8 scoops vanilla ice cream
4 scoops coffee ice cream
Reduced-fat spray cream
4 cat's tongue cookies
16 tablespoons cold coffee
4 ice cubes
4 straws

- Prepare a small cup of coffee and leave to cool. Put the ice cubes in a freezer bag and crush finely by pounding.
- Compose the Café liégeois at the last moment. In each ice-cream bowl, pour 4 tablespoons of cold coffee, then add a handful of crushed ice. Place 2 scoops of vanilla and 1 scoop of coffee ice cream in each. Top each with whipped cream and a cookie.
- Insert a straw and serve.

Chestnut Cream

“ CRÈME DE MARRONS ”

SERVE **4**
PREPARATION **1 hour**
COOKING **45 min**

3 lb (1 ½ kg) chestnuts
2 lb (1 kg) sugar
1 ½ glasses water
1 vanilla pod

- Make a slit across the rounded side of each chestnut.
- Place the chestnuts in a saucepan. Cover well with cold water, then boil for several minutes.
- Take off the heat, then take 2 or 3 chestnuts at a time while leaving the others in the saucepan of hot water. Remove the chestnut shells. Little by little, add the shelled chestnuts into a saucepan with 1 pint (½ liter) of warm water. Cover and cook over low heat for several minutes. They are cooked when they can be mashed easily.
- Drain the chestnuts, and using a blender, blend until very smooth. Keep warm.
- Make a syrup by heating the sugar and water together, stirring to dissolve the sugar. The syrup has reached the right consistency (“*au petit boulé*”) if a drop of syrup, dropped into cold water, forms a small, malleable ball. Pour the syrup onto the hot puree. Add the vanilla pod. Heat gently while stirring. Leave to boil for 15 to 20 minutes. The mixture should become thick and cling to a spoon. Remove the vanilla pod.
- Place into jars and invert.

Chocolate Fondant Cake

“ FONDANT AU CHOCOLAT ”

SERVE **4**
PREPARATION **10 min**
COOKING **25 min**

5 oz (150 g) dark chocolate
3 eggs
2 ¾ oz (80 g) butter, cut into pieces
1 ¾ oz (50 g) sugar
1 oz (30 g) flour
Several raspberries to decorate

- Preheat the oven to 400 °F (200 °C / gas mark 7).
- In a saucepan, melt the chocolate and butter over very low heat.
- In a large bowl, combine the sugar, eggs, flour and chocolate. Mix well.
- Butter and flour a cake mold and pour in the batter.
- Bake for around 10 to 11 minutes. It's perfectly normal for the cake to appear not quite cooked when you take it out of the oven. Leave it to cool, then unmold it. Decorate with a handful of raspberries.

Chocolate *Mousse*

“ MOUSSE AU CHOCOLAT ”

SERVE **4**
PREPARATION **15 min**

4 ½ oz (130 g) chocolate
1 nob butter
4 egg whites
3 egg yolks
1 pinch salt

- Melt the chocolate with the nob of butter.
- Take off the heat when a liquid is obtained.
- Break the eggs, separating the whites from the yolks.
- Pour 3 yolks into the saucepan of melted chocolate while stirring energetically (to prevent the yolks from cooking).
- Add a pinch of salt to the egg whites, then beat until stiff peaks form.
- Combine a little of the beaten egg whites with the chocolate and mix energetically until well combined.
- Then, very gently fold in the rest of the egg whites, using a wooden spoon.
- Refrigerate for at least 3 hours before serving.

Cinnamon Apple-Pear Compote

“ COMPOTE POMMES POIRES CANNELLE ”

SERVE **4**
PREPARATION **10 min**
COOKING **20 min**

4 apples
2 ripe pears
½ glass water
1 tablespoon sugar
2 pinches cinnamon

- Peel and deseed the apples and pears. Cut into cubes.
- Place the fruits, sugar and cinnamon into a saucepan and add the water.
- Cover the saucepan and simmer over low heat for 20 minutes. Stir regularly.
- Blend everything with a mixer and leave to cool at room temperature.
- You may like to replace the cinnamon with Bourbon vanilla. Serve lukewarm or cold with small cookies.

Crème *Brûlée*

SERVE **4**
PREPARATION **15 min**
COOKING **1 hour**

5 egg yolks
3 ½ oz (100 g) sugar
1 pt (50 cl) single cream
1 vanilla pod

- Whip the egg yolks with the sugar in a bowl until the mixture pales in color and becomes very foamy.
- Split the vanilla pod in half lengthwise and scrape out the seeds with a knife, directly into the bowl, then mix.
- Add the single cream little by little while whisking energetically.
- Pour the mixture into four individual ramekins and bake in an oven preheated to 210 °F (100 °C / gas mark 3) for around 1 hour. Leave to cool at room temperature, then keep refrigerated for around 2 hours to set.
- To finish, caramelize the desserts just before serving by sprinkling sugar on top, then using a blowtorch. If you don't have a blowtorch, place them under a very hot oven grill for several seconds. When using the grill, place the desserts in the freezer 15 to 20 minutes beforehand.

Crème Caramel

SERVE **4**
PREPARATION **15 min**
COOKING **45 min**

1 pt (50 cl) milk
2 whole eggs + 2 egg yolks
3 ½ oz (100 g) sugar
1 teaspoon vanilla essence
1 teaspoon vanilla sugar
1 pt (50 cl) liquid caramel

- Heat the milk with the vanilla essence.
- In a large bowl, place the 2 eggs, 2 egg yolks and sugar. Beat until the mixture pales in color.
- When the milk is hot, pour it into the mixture in the bowl, and stir in.
- Pour liquid caramel onto the bottom of four individual ramekins, then fill the ramekins with the mixture.
- Place the ramekins in an oven dish. Prepare a bain-marie by adding water to the oven dish so that it comes halfway up the ramekins' height.
- Place in the oven at 350 °F (180 °C / gas mark 6) for 45 minutes. Check if set by piercing the mixture with the tip of a knife.
- Leave to cool before refrigerating.

Crêpes Suzette

SERVE **4**
PREPARATION **35 min**
COOKING **30 min**

For the crêpe batter:

4 ½ oz (130 g) flour
1 egg
1 egg yolk
1 cup (25 cl) milk
2 oz (60 g) butter
1 teaspoon superfine sugar
1 pinch salt

For the garnish:

3 mandarins + several segments to decorate
1 tablespoon superfine sugar
1 tablespoon icing sugar
2 ½ oz (70 g) butter
4 tablespoons Curacao
2 tablespoons cognac

- **For the crêpe batter:** mix 1 ounce (30 grams) of butter with the flour, egg, egg yolk, superfine sugar, salt and milk.
- Cook 12 very thin crêpes in the remaining ounce (30 grams) of butter. Set aside in the oven preheated to 140 °F (60 °C / gas mark 2).
- **For the the garnish:** cut the zests of the mandarins into thin slices and squeeze their juice.
- Mix the melted butter with the icing sugar until you obtain a foamy mixture.
- Combine half of the mandarin juice and zests to the mixture.
- Spread the garnish onto a crêpe. Then fold the crepe into four and place on a pan. Repeat with remaining crêpes.
- Moisten the crêpes with the rest of the mandarin juice combined with the remaining zest and superfine sugar.
- Heat on a stove.
- As soon as the juice starts to bubble, drizzle the crêpes with the cognac and Curacao, mixed together.
- Flambé the crêpes, then decorate them with the mandarin segments.

Dame Blanche Ice Cream

“ DAME BLANCHE ”

SERVE **4**
PREPARATION **10 min**

5 oz (150 g) dark cooking chocolate

4 scoops vanilla ice cream

Sweetened whipped cream

4 cigarette cookies (optional)

- Melt the chocolate in a bain-marie.
- Place a scoop of vanilla ice cream in each bowl.
- Cover with the melted chocolate.
- Decorate each bowl with whipped cream and a cookie, and serve.

Fine Chocolate Tartlets

“ TARTE FINE AU CHOCOLAT ”

SERVE **4**
PREPARATION **30 min**
COOKING **20 min**

For the sweet shortcrust pastry:

2 oz (60 g) butter
1 ¼ oz (35 g) icing sugar
½ oz (15 g) almond meal
1 egg
4 oz (110 g) flour
Salt

For the chocolate cream:

3 ½ oz (100 g) 70% cacao dark chocolate
5 oz (140 g) crème fraîche
2 tablespoons milk
1 oz (30 g) superfine sugar

For the sweet shortcrust pastry:

- Place the softened butter into a mixing bowl, then add the icing sugar, almond meal, half of the egg and a pinch of salt.
- Combine quickly, adding the flour little by little, and kneading the dough as little as possible. Let the dough rest in the refrigerator for at least 2 hours.
- Roll out the pastry to fill 4 tartlet molds. Bake in the oven at 350 °F (180 °C / gas mark 6) for 10 minutes.

For the chocolate cream:

- Finely chop the chocolate with a knife and melt gently using a bain-marie.
- In a saucepan, bring the crème fraîche and superfine sugar to a simmer, and pour the mixture over the melted chocolate. Stir in.
- Mix the milk and the rest of the egg, then combine with the chocolate cream.
- Pour this mixture into the pastry bases and bake at 350 °F (180 °C / gas mark 6) for 10 minutes.
- Serve warm.

Floating *Island*

“ ÎLE FLOTTANTE ”

SERVE **4**
PREPARATION **20 min**
COOKING **15 min**

For the crème anglaise:

4 egg yolks

1 pt (50 cl) milk

2 oz (60 g) sugar

1 sachet vanilla sugar

For the floating islands:

4 egg whites

1 ½ oz (40 g) sugar (1/3 oz / 10 g per egg white)

1 pinch salt

For the caramel:

1 ¾ oz (50 g sugar)

For the crème anglaise:

- Boil the milk with the vanilla sugar in a saucepan. Beat the egg yolks and sugar energetically in a bowl until the mixture pales in color and becomes quite thick.
- Little by little, gently pour the milk into the sugar-egg mixture while stirring. Pour the whole mixture back into the saucepan and thicken by cooking for 7 minutes over low heat, stirring continuously with a wooden spoon.
- Take the cream off the heat immediately, then pour into a large bowl to cool. Set aside, keeping refrigerated.

For the floating islands:

- Beat the egg whites with a pinch of salt until stiff peaks form, adding the sugar in two stages.
- In a large saucepan, simmer 2 pints (1 liter) of water. Gently add the sugared egg white to the simmering water, one spoonful at a time. Cook for 20 seconds on each side. Remove immediately from the water and drain on a kitchen towel. Leave to cool.

For the caramel:

- Heat the sugar (without water) on a gentle heat until it melts and takes on an attractive amber color.
- When it's mealtime, fill the dessert bowls with crème anglaise, add 1 or 2 islands, then top lightly with the caramel coulis.

Fontainebleau

SERVE **4**
PREPARATION **20 min**

10 oz (300 g) faisselle (a type of fresh cheese)

1 ¼ cups (30 cl) full-fat single cream

1 oz (30 g) icing sugar

1 vanilla pod

Red-fruit coulis (optional)

Toasted flaked almonds (optional)

- Place the faisselle into a sieve, itself placed at the bottom of a recipient. Cover with plastic wrap and put a weight (not too heavy) on top to help the liquid flow out. Refrigerate for at least 2 hours (or even overnight if you like).
- Whip up a classic Chantilly cream: pour the full-fat single cream into a well-chilled large bowl. Place the bowl in your kitchen sink, filled with very cold water, and start whisking steadily and energetically, without stopping. When the whisk begins to leave visible traces on the cream, sprinkle in the icing sugar and continue whisking. The cream is ready when it forms a small peak like a bird's beak as you lift the whisk from it.
- Slice the vanilla pod open lengthways and scrape out the seeds with the help of a knife. Add the vanilla seeds to the Chantilly and gently fold into the faisselle.
- Bear in mind: the folding motion helps to prevent air from being knocked out of the Chantilly cream.
- You can cover the dessert with a red-fruit coulis and sprinkle over toasted flaked almonds.

Lemon Meringue Tart

“ TARTE AU CITRON MERINGUÉE ”

SERVE **4**
PREPARATION **30 min**
COOKING **25 min**

For the lemon cream:

- 2 lemons
- 4 whole eggs
- 7 oz (120 g) sugar
- 2 ½ oz (70 g) butter, cut into small pieces

For the sweet shortcrust pastry:

- 6 oz (170 g) flour
- 3 oz (85 g) unsalted butter
- 1 ½ oz (40 g) superfine sugar
- 2 egg yolks
- 2 ½ tablespoons (3.5 cl) water
- 1 pinch salt

For the meringue:

- 2 egg whites
- 3 ½ oz (100 g) sugar

For the sweet shortcrust pastry:

- Preheat the oven to 350 °F (180 °C / gas mark 6). Beat the egg yolks and sugar with a little water till pale in color (set aside the egg whites). Use your fingers to combine the flour and butter, cut into small pieces, till you obtain a sandy texture. Make a well in the middle of the flour-butter sand and pour the liquid mixture into the middle. Form a ball with your palms and knead once or twice. Roll out the pastry directly onto a piece of greaseproof paper. Prick the dough with a fork and place it, with the paper, into a pie dish. Then place more greaseproof paper on top of the dough and cover it with dried beans (so that the pastry remains smooth and even underneath). Bake “blind” this way for 10 minutes (the pastry should not brown—or very little).

For the lemon cream:

- Wash and dry the lemons, and remove the zest with a peeler. Cut the lemons in half, then squeeze them and set aside the juice.
- In a large bowl, beat the eggs with the sugar.
- In a saucepan, melt the butter and combine with the lemon juice and zests. Add the beaten eggs, then cook while stirring with a whisk. Bring to a boil and cook until the cream thickens (around 3 minutes). Garnish the pastry base with this cream, then refrigerate to set the lemon cream.

For the meringue:

- Pour the two egg whites into a large bowl with half the sugar. Beat the egg whites until stiff peaks form, then continue beating while adding the rest of the sugar. Place the meringue preparation into a pastry bag to decorate the tart. To brown the meringue, two options are available: using a kitchen blowtorch or placing under the oven grill for several seconds.

Millefeuille

SERVE **4**
PREPARATION **30 min**
COOKING **25 min**

2 packs puff pastry

For the crème pâtissière:

3 eggs
2 pt (1 l) milk
1 oz (30 g) sugar
3 1/3 oz (95 g) flour
1 vanilla pod or 1 sachet vanilla sugar
1 ¾ oz (50 g) butter

For the icing:

1 oz (30 g) icing sugar
Coffee extract or chocolate
Water

- Spread out the pastry sheets and cut out 3 rectangles of the same size. To do so, you can place one pastry sheet on top of the other, or else fold the sheets. Prick the pastry sheets with a fork.
- Place the rectangles next to one another on a baking sheet, and place a pie dish on top of them to apply pressure. Bake for 15 minutes at 350 °F (180 °C / gas mark 6).
- **For the crème pâtissière:** While the baking is going on, in a large bowl, whisk together the eggs, sugar, vanilla seeds scraped out from the pod (or vanilla sugar), and flour. Boil the milk, making sure that it doesn't stick to the bottom of the saucepan. When the milk is at a boil, pour it immediately into the bowl. Combine with the bowl's contents, then pour back into the saucepan and cook for several minutes (2 to 3 minutes) until the liquid takes on the consistency of a cream.
- Pour the cream into a cold bowl and beat with an electric beater while adding the butter, little by little, until the texture is smooth and glossy. Until the crème pâtissière is needed, keep it covered with plastic wrap to prevent a skin from forming on its surface.
- When the pastry rectangles are cooked and have cooled a little, place one rectangle on the worktop, and spread with crème pâtissière using a flat metallic spatula. Place on top the second rectangle. Press down so that they stick together. Spread a second layer of crème pâtissière. Finally, place the last pastry rectangle on top. Wait until the millefeuille is cold to add the icing.

- **For the icing:** place the icing sugar in a large bowl. Add a tablespoon of water and mix. Keep adding water until all the icing sugar is mixed in and the mixture is not too thin.
- If there is not enough icing to cover the cake, prepare more. Set aside a little icing and mix with the coffee extract or melted chocolate.
- Quickly pour the white icing over the millefeuille and spread evenly on top with the flat spatula. Then, immediately after, using a stencil or syringe with a nozzle, trace parallel lines on the millefeuille with the colored icing.
- With the tip of a knife, draw another set of parallel lines—this time, perpendicular to the first set of colored lines—, first in one direction, then the other.
- Trim the edges of the millefeuille for a neat, sharp presentation. Keep refrigerated until serving.

Paris-Brest

SERVE **4**
PREPARATION **45 min**
COOKING **1 hour**

For the choux pastry:

1 cup (25 cl) water
1 cup (25 cl) full-fat milk
8 oz (225 g) semi-salted butter
½ oz (15 g) sugar
9 ¾ oz (275 g) flour
8 eggs
1 ¾ oz (50 g) flaked almonds

For the praline crème mousseline:

1 pt (50 cl) milk
4 ½ oz (130 g) praline
6 egg yolks
5 oz (150 g) sugar
1 ¾ oz (50 g) cornstarch
9 oz (250 g) butter
Icing sugar

For the choux pastry:

- Preheat the oven to 300 °F (150 °C / gas mark 5).
- In a saucepan, combine the water, milk, butter and sugar. Heat to melt the butter, then stir in the flour and let the mixture dry out on the stove for around 3 minutes. Off the heat, in a large bowl, add the eggs, one by one, to the mixture, mixing with a spatula until a smooth pastry forms. The pastry should pull away from the side of the bowl.
- Place the choux pastry into a pastry bag with a plain nozzle, and pipe a ring of pastry, roughly 20 cm in diameter, on an oven tray covered with a sheet of parchment paper. Then pipe a second ring, inside the first one and touching it, then a third one overlapping the first two. Scatter with flaked almonds.
- Bake for 40 to 45 minutes. Cool.

For the praline crème mousseline:

- In a saucepan, mix the milk and praline.
- Beat the egg yolks with the sugar till they pale in color. Add the cornstarch. Pour into the praline-milk mixture in the saucepan and cook until boiling. Take off the heat and add 1 ¾ ounces (50 grams) of butter. Transfer the cream into a large bowl, cover with plastic wrap and leave to cool (around 1 hour).
- In the meantime, leave the remaining butter at room temperature so that it softens.
- Once the cream has cooled, beat it with an electric beater and little by little, combine with the 7 ounces (200 grams) of softened butter.
- Slice the choux pastry ring in half, dividing the top from the base. Garnish the base with the praline crème mousseline, using a pastry bag. Sandwich the filling with the top of the ring. Sprinkle with icing sugar and serve.

Pears *Belle Hélène*

“ POIRES BELLE HÉLÈNE ”

SERVE **4**
PREPARATION **15 min**
COOKING **20 min**

4 just-ripe pears
3 ½ oz (100 g) superfine sugar
3 ½ oz (100 g) dark chocolate
2 pt (1 l) water
Flaked almonds

- Peel the pears with a peeler, leaving the stem.
- Make a syrup with water and sugar. If you like, you can flavor the syrup with vanilla sugar or spices (e.g. cinnamon, ginger).
- Boil and poach the pears in the syrup for 10 to 15 minutes till very tender. Place them in the individual dessert bowls.
- Let the pears cool. To bring out the contrast between hot and cold, you can refrigerate the pears for half an hour before serving (but no more as they risk becoming too cold).
- 10 minutes before serving, melt the chocolate very gently using a bain-marie, till it becomes completely liquid. It may be helpful to add a tablespoon of syrup to obtain the desired degree of liquidity.
- Cover the pears with the chocolate.
- To decorate, add some toasted flaked almonds, crisped in a frying pan beforehand.
- Serve immediately while the chocolate is still steaming.

Profiteroles

SERVE **4**
PREPARATION **20 min**
COOKING **20 min**

For the choux pastry:

½ pt (¼ l) water
3 ½ oz (100 g) butter
1 pinch salt
7 oz (200 g) flour
4 eggs

For the chocolate sauce:

10 ½ oz (300 g) dark chocolate
1 ¾ oz (50 g) sugar
1 cup (25 cl) milk
1 pt (½ l) vanilla ice cream

For the choux pastry:

- Heat the water in a saucepan with the butter and salt, and bring to a boil. Add the flour off the stove, and mix with a wooden spatula. Place back on the stove, over medium heat, stirring continuously until the pastry pulls away from the sides of the saucepan. Leave to cool and add the eggs one by one. Using two spoons, form little walnut-sized balls and place on a baking sheet (spacing them out well). Bake at 350 °F (180 °C / gas mark 6) for 20 minutes. Leave to cool.

For the chocolate sauce:

- Bring the milk to a boil in a saucepan with the chocolate, cut into squares, and the sugar. Mix well.
- When the choux pastries are cooked (puffed up nicely), let them cool for a few minutes, then cut them in half so as to obtain a top and a base.
- Stuff them with vanilla ice cream and cover with chocolate sauce. Serve immediately.

Rice *Pudding*

“ RIZ AU LAIT ”

SERVE **4**
PREPARATION **15 min**
COOKING **1 ½ hour**

4 ½ oz (130 g) short—or medium—grain rice
2 pt (1 l) milk
1 ½ oz (40 g) sugar
1 vanilla pod

- Slice the vanilla pod in half lengthwise, and drop into a saucepan with the milk. Heat the milk.
- Rinse the rice in water, then add to the saucepan when the milk begins to boil.
- Cover the saucepan and cook over very low heat for between 70 and 90 minutes. A word of advice: don't stir the rice while it's cooking.
- 10 minutes before the rice finishes cooking, pour the sugar into the saucepan and stir. When you lift the lid to pour in the sugar, you will see that the rice has "swollen up"—this is normal.
- When the rice has finished cooking, remove the vanilla pod. Pour the rice into a bowl and leave to cool. Serve at room temperature.

Rum Baba

“ BABA AU RHUM ”

SERVE **4**
PREPARATION **10 min**
COOKING **30 min**

4 ½ oz (130 g) superfine sugar
3 eggs
1 ¾ oz (50 g) butter, melted
4 1/3 oz (125 g) flour
1 sachet baking powder

For the syrup:
8 oz (225 g) sugar
18 tablespoons (30 cl) water
6 tablespoons (10 cl) rum

- Preheat the oven to 350 °F (180 °C / gas mark 6) and grease a rum baba mold.
- Blend the sugar and eggs with an electric beater or food processor, then add the melted butter, flour, baking powder and blend until the batter is smooth.
- Pour the batter into the mold and bake for 15 minutes. Lower the temperature to 300 °F (150 °C / gas mark 4) and cook for another 15 minutes.
- Prepare the syrup: in a saucepan, bring to a boil the water and sugar, then add the rum. Leave to simmer gently for 3 minutes.
- Unmold the baba into a deep dish. Using a ladle, pour the syrup over the cake until it is well soaked. For an extra touch of indulgence, you can cover the baba with whipped cream.

Tarte *Tatin*

SERVE **4**
PREPARATION **30 min**
COOKING **40 min**

5 Golden Delicious or Granny Smith apples

1 pack pure-butter puff pastry

1 ½ sachets vanilla sugar

Cinnamon

2 1/3 oz (65 g) butter

2 1/3 oz (65 g) superfine sugar

- Preheat the oven to 350 °F (180 °C / gas mark 6).
- Melt the butter in a round non-stick pie dish placed directly on the stove.
- Add the superfine sugar and lower the heat to make caramel.
- Peel the 5 apples, leaving them whole. Cut in half and remove the core while preserving the half shapes. Put the cored halves back together and arrange in a ring on the pie dish, with one or two apples in the middle of the ring. Flatten the apples with a spatula from time to time while they poach in the caramel, which should be golden in color (and not be allowed to blacken).
- Scatter the apples with vanilla sugar and cinnamon.
- Take the dish off the heat and cover with the sheet of puff pastry, pressing down the edges firmly.
- Bake for 35 to 40 minutes.
- Invert onto a deep serving platter so that the apples are on top, the pastry on the bottom, and serve warm.

Toutes les photos sont © Shutterstock

Édition : Mathilde Kressmann
Traduction : Fui Lee Luk
Relecture : Aude Gandiol et Olivier Debanne

Direction artistique et réalisation : Isabelle Chemin

Achevé d'imprimé en UE mai 2018
Dépôt légal : juin 2018

ISBN : 978-2-37395-044-1